501
Excuses
For A Bad
Golf Shot

Justin J. Exner

ISBN: 0-9665319-1-4

Library of Congress Number: 99-60046

© 2000 Justin J. Exner

Illustrations by Dawn M. Emerson

Layout by Francine Smith

Edited by Gayle Breunig

Visit us on the web at www.501excuses.com

Printed in 2000 by Greenleaf Enterprises, Inc. in Cleveland, Ohio

2000 First Edition, Second Printing

I dedicate this book to my family, with special thanks to my mother Janet.
I love you all.

In addition, I would like to thank those who believed in me and especially those who did not.

Please support your local charities.
It does make a difference.

Justin Exner earned a B.A. in Aviation Business from Embry Riddle Aeronautical University in Daytona Beach FL. After graduation, he began work as a baggage handler for a national air carrier. In 1998, he received his MBA from Franklin University in Columbus, OH. He spends most of his free time traveling and hunting for little white balls in forests.

There is no excuse for a bad golf shot, but...

[1]

A drop of sweat fell in my eye and
I missed the ball.

. . . .

[2]

I stubbed my toe on the base of
my bed, now I can't wear my golf shoes.

. . . .

[3]

I've only played with these
clubs twice.

. . . .

[4]

My rain suit is too tight and I can't
swing my club smoothly.

. . . .

[5]

My ball is all scuffed up.

. . . .

"Bad Lie"

[6]

I keep picking up my head. I'm afraid the geese are
going to do their business on me.

. . . .

[7]

The tee was leaning too far forward.

. . . .

[8]

I get nervous shooting last all the time.

. . . .

[9]

The sun was in my eyes.

. . . .

[10]

I thought we were using the green over there.

. . . .

[11]

My dog chewed up my golf glove... Now my club slips.

. . . .

[12]
The curvature of the earth caused my putt
to move away from its intended target.

. . . .

[13]
I hit it off the heel of the club.

. . . .

[14]
My clubs need to be re-gripped. They keep
slipping out of my hand.

. . . .

[15]
I'm missing some spikes on my golf
shoes and it causes me to slip.

. . . .

[16]
I thought this was the nine iron, not the six.

. . . .

[17]

It's this new putter. I can't get a feel for it.

. . . .

[18]

The hole was in a different spot when
I scouted the course this morning.

. . . .

[19]

I thought you said "dog leg left."

. . . .

[20]

The golfers on the other tee box were
talking and I couldn't concentrate.

. . . .

[21]

The ball washer was out of water. I couldn't focus with
the speck of dirt on the ball.

. . . .

[22]

The wind held the ball up in the air. I knew I should have gone to church instead.

8

[23]

I have tendonitis in my left foot.

. . . .

[24]

It's my first time playing golf this year.

. . . .

[25]

I forgot my sunglasses in my other golf bag.

. . . .

[26]

These are my wife's clubs. Mine are
being re-gripped.

. . . .

[27]

It must have kicked the wrong
way off of the hill because the
shot looked perfect.

. . . .

"Gust of Wind"

[28]

I didn't follow through on the swing.

. . . .

[29]

It's just too hot to be playing golf, I can't focus.

. . . .

[30]

My clubs are too short. You know I grew
two inches since I played last week.

. . . .

[31]

My ball isn't white. I can only play
with white golf balls.

. . . .

[32]

That pond wasn't there last week.

. . . .

[33]

My caddie gave me the wrong club.

. . . .

[34]

My knee hurts from my old high school football injury.

. . . .

[35]

I didn't follow through with my hips.

. . . .

[36]

I'm doing exactly what my golf instructor told me to do, but the ball keeps slicing.

. . . .

[37]

That rock deflected my putt to the left.

. . . .

[38]

**I focus my attention on putting,
not on my drives.**

. . . .

[39]

**I had too big of a breakfast.
I can't get the club around my gut.**

. . . .

[40]

**The greens-keeper hasn't mowed the green this week.
Now the greens are too slow.**

. . . .

13

[41]

That tree wasn't there last year. This is a conspiracy.

. . . .

[42]

I just didn't get all of the ball.

. . . .

[43]

My dog urinated on my good golf shoes so I
have to play in my sneakers.

. . . .

[44]

There is a nick on my ball so it spun out of bounds.

. . . .

[45]

I play better with golfers who are actually good.

. . . .

[46]

These are new clubs.

. . . .

[47]

I took too much of the earth on that swing.

. . . .

[48]

The pin placement was different yesterday.
It almost seems like they change it everyday.

. . . .

[49]
That was supposed to be a practice swing.

. . . .

[50]
I normally hit a bucket of balls before playing.

. . . .

[51]
My clubs were lost by the airline.
I'm having to use rentals.

. . . .

[52]
Those hedges were just planted.
That's a do-over.

. . . .

[53]
This course does not have the
yardage marked accurately.
There is no way that was 139 yards.

. . . .

[54]

The group ahead of us is playing too slow.
It's throwing off my rythym.

. . . .

[55]

I can't play on this course. I haven't
been able to practice it on virtual golf.

. . . .

[56]

No one has replaced their ball marks on the green, and
my putt keeps angling off course.

. . . .

[57]

I hit it off the toe of the club.

. . . .

[58]

I forgot my golf visor in the car.

. . . .

"Triple Bogey"

[59]

It is just too cold to play golf.

. . . .

[60]

I didn't have lunch. I have no energy.

. . . .

[61]

My socks are wet from the rain.
I keep slipping in my shoes.

. . . .

[62]

These are new golf shoes.

. . . .

[63]

I quit smoking yesterday.

. . . .

[64]

That leaf rolled in front of my putt.

. . . .

[65]

It must have been that last beer. I had a great round going.

[66]

I couldn't see from back there that it was
not a vertical water hazard.

. . . .

[67]

I am allergic to the pesticide spray. My eyes are
watering and I can't see the ball.

. . . .

[68]

Since canceling my subscription for Golf
Digest, I just don't play well.

. . . .

[69]

The putting green was closed this morning.

. . . .

[70]

I was thrown off the tour, so I haven't
been able to play regularly.

. . . .

[71]

I lost one of my contacts and
the flagstick is all fuzzy.

. . . .

[72]

If the pin was pulled, it would have gone Gust of
Windin.

. . . .

[73]

I thought I could ask what club you use
without taking penalty strokes.

. . . .

[74]

I thought you get a Mulligan every hole.
That's the way I was taught.

. . . .

[75]

My golf glove is wet. I can't get
a grip on the club.

. . . .

"Blind Shot!"

[76]
The green sloped differently last year.

. . . .

[77]
The driving range uses a different type of
golf ball, I can't gauge my distance.

. . . .

[78]
The golf cart ran over my ball and plugged it.

. . . .

[79]
The ground is too dry. My divots are
not coming off smoothly.

. . . .

[80]
I have been living in Africa the last three years and no
courses are within walking distance.

. . . .

[81]

I've been working on my MBA. I just
haven't had time to practice.

. . . .

[82]

I'm too busy at work to get
away and play. I'm inconsistent.

. . . .

[83]

My wife won't let me play since having the kid. I knew I
should have gotten a dog instead.

. . . .

[84]

The driving range was closed.

. . . .

[85]

I'm having trouble adjusting to these
left-handed clubs, but I did save $20.

. . . .

[86]

My back is sunburned. It hurts to swing.

. . . .

[87]

I'm hung over from the 18 holes yesterday.

. . . .

[88]

The nearest golf course is two hundred
miles from my house.

. . . .

[89]

My rain suit is at home. I don't play
well while wearing wet clothes.

. . . .

[90]

My wife is pregnant and I can't get
any sleep-she nags and eats constantly.

. . . .

[91]

*A fly landed on my ball
right when I hit.*

[92]

I have tennis elbow.
What the heck is tennis elbow anyway?

. . . .

[93]

That sunflower seed threw off my putt.

. . . .

[94]

I have had to play softball every Saturday and Sunday
this summer. I just haven't been out.

. . . .

[95]

I haven't had any money to play.
my school loans are due.

. . . .

[96]

I always get kicked off the course for
being intoxicated. This is the first round
I've finished.

. . . .

[97]

The sun screen I put on my hands made
them greasy and my club slipped.

. . . .

[98]

I have a tear in my golf glove.

. . . .

[99]

I can't play with graphite shafts.
Steel is the way to go.

. . . .

[100]

The course doesn't let you chip on
the practice green.

. . . .

[101]

My short game is not what I focused
on in my last lesson.

. . . .

"The Optimist"

[102]

I left my watch on and it throws
off my balance.

. . . .

[103]

I haven't taken putting lessons yet.

. . . .

[104]

I ran out off tees, so I had to use half a tee and
I couldn't get the loft required to fly the trap.

. . . .

[105]

I cut my hand at work, so I can't get
a firm grip on the clubs - but I love sick leave.

. . . .

[106]

I have a headache from the concert last night.
I just can't concentrate.

. . . .

[107]

That bird deflected my shot into the woods.
I hope my ball isn't scuffed.

. . . .

[108]

I thought this was a par 5.
I was laying up for par.

. . . .

[109]

A squirrel pushed my ball into the trap, the good-for-nothing wannabe rats.

. . . .

[110]

I'm tired because I usually never walk.

. . . .

[111]

It rained all week and I couldn't practice.

. . . .

[112]

I've only been golfing 20 years.
I don't have my swing down yet.

. . . .

[113]

I thought this was a dog leg left.
It looks that way from the score card.

. . . .

[114]

You should have told me about the
water on this hole.

. . . .

115]

I never played this course before, so I'm
not familiar with the layout.

. . . .

[116]

I don't have a sand wedge.
I lost it in the lake last time I played.

. . . .

[117]

I didn't open my stance and I pushed
the ball to the left.

. . . .

[118]

My shoes aren't tied tight enough.

. . . .

[119]

Someone stole my other clubs because I forgot to set
the alarm on my golf bag.

. . . .

[120]

I'm afraid I'll kill another bird - I just
can't get over the fear.

. . . .

[121]

I forgot my antacid and I have bad indigestion from
eating all that candy last night.

. . . .

"Not Quite Past the Red Tees"

[122]

Those guys were making too much
noise in the other fairway.

. . . .

[123]

I usually play from the blue tees.
Being this close confuses me.

. . . .

[124]

This wasn't considered out of
bounds last year.

. . . .

[125]

The greens are much faster in Florida.

. . . .

[126]

I left my pitching wedge in
the lake over there.

. . . .

[127]

I pushed my hips too much while trying
to get out of that fairway trap.

. . . .

[128]

The ball should go left if the ball is
above my feet.

. . . .

[129]

I can't keep my head still on the back swing.

. . . .

[130]

I moved my body too far forward on impact and sliced it into
the fairway but it rolled into the woods.

. . . .

[131]

I have a bad case of jet lag.

. . . .

[132]

My other driver has a 11.5 degree loft.
I can't hit a 9 degree driver.

. . . .

[133]

I didn't keep my left arm in. I hate this game.

. . . .

[134]

I gripped the club too far down and
topped the ball.

. . . .

[135]

I just can't keep my mind off of her, it's so
frustrating. Where is the beer girl anyway?

. . . .

[136]

I just keep pushing the ball.
I don't know what the hell is wrong.

. . . .

[137]

These greens have way too much sand on them. It
slows down all my putts.

. . . .

[138]

Your farts stink. I can't concentrate,
let alone breathe.

. . . .

[139]

I didn't have fish for breakfast - I only play well
when I eat fish for breakfast.

. . . .

[140]

The ranger keeps following me around. I can't
focus when I'm being watched.

. . . .

[141]

I ate way too much on the turn,
now I'm bloated. I need a port-a-pottie.

. . . .

[142]

The hail keeps getting in my eyes. Maybe we should
wait until the storm passes.

. . . .

[143]

The balls fly much further in Colorado.
I can't get my distance gauged.

. . . .

[144]

My wrists aren't breaking on impact.

. . . .

[145]

I have a bad back from rugby
practice yesterday.

. . . .

[146]

Those airplanes are flying too low.
The exhaust pushed my ball into the water.

. . . .

[147]

That bee must be addicted to my cologne.
It keeps following me from hole to hole.

. . . .

[148]

The fairway looks like it slopes to the left, not the
right.

. . . .

[149]

My hands are too far to the
left on my grip.

. . . .

[150]

I keep closing the club face and
I can't get the loft to clear the red tees.

. . . .

[151]

My old caddy's notes are in Japanese and
I can't interpret them since he was deported.

. . . .

"Slow Play"

[152]

I pulled a muscle in my leg while helping
an elderly lady get her bag out of the car trunk.

. . . .

[153]

I lost all my money gambling and now
I can't afford lessons.

. . . .

[154]

My wife was awarded my
balls in the divorce.

. . . .

[155]

My grip just isn't comfortable.

. . . .

[156]

I hurt my hips while having
sex last night.

. . . .

[157]

Those swing machines are too expensive.

. . . .

[158]

I slept on my shoulder the wrong way. Now my swing is
all messed up

. . . .

[159]

I wanted to practice, but the range was out of balls.

. . . .

43

[160]

I focus too much on where the ball is going.
I can never follow through.

. . . .

[161]

The sand trap should not be right in the
middle of the fairway. Oh, I thought that
was our fairway.

. . . .

[162]

Damn it, have you no etiquette? Please quit breathing when I swing.

[163]

The instructor told me to play my slice and now I hit the ball straight.

. . . .

[164]

I made it over the lake last time. It must be the humidity

. . . .

[165]

The sand is much heavier in Scotland.

. . . .

[166]

The wind keeps shifting when I hit.

. . . .

[167]

I pulled the putter too far back.

. . . .

"Runaway Ball"

[168]

I duffed the shot. No excuse for that.

. . . .

[169]

I'm just not releasing on the ball.

. . . .

[170]

I hurt my elbow when I got out of that
damn cart.

. . . .

[171]

My chiropractor is out of town.
I can't get loose.

. . . .

[172]

I lined up with the ball too close
to my left foot.

. . . .

[173]

These balls don't fly as far as yours,
but I got a good deal on mine.

. . . .

[174]

When I'm on the practice tee the ball
always goes straight.

. . . .

[175]

Didn't you hear that sound in the woods
during my swing? It sounded like a duck.
What's that smell?

. . . .

[176]

My swing looks perfect on video,
I don't know what's wrong.

. . . .

[177]

I just need to work on my grip.

. . . .

[178]

I just don't have any rhythym today.
I need to listen to some music.

. . . .

[179]

I forgot about that trap in
front of the green.

. . . .

[180]

I am hitting the ball too perfectly.
It keeps going too far.

. . . .

[181]

I keep pulling the ball.
It must be the aerobics I've been taking.

. . . .

[182]

Damn it! Damn it! Damn it!

. . . .

[183]

I needed to use a seven, not an eight,
just short of a hole in one.

. . . .

[184]

I'm getting out of the box fine – it's my
short game that is so bad.

. . . .

[185]

When I yelled "fore", my caddie thought
that was the club I needed.

. . . .

[186]

I play better with women. They
motivate me.

. . . .

[187]

I decided to become celibate
yesterday.

. . . .

[188]

Someone left a cigar burning on the
green and it made my putt drift.

. . . .

[189]

I hate these soft spikes. I keep slipping.

. . . .

[190]

I played the ball too far back in my stance and
I couldn't get it over that tree.

. . . .

[191]

I always lift my head when I chip. I need to
tie a hook around my privates and a noose around my
neck. I'll never look up again.

. . . .

[192]

These balatas spin too much. I like a
harder shelled ball.

. . . .

[193]

My back-swing is way too short.

. . . .

[194]

I was up all night watching "MASH" reruns.
I didn't get any rest.

. . . .

195]

I took too much sand on that swing.

. . . .

[196]

You are never watching when
I hit a good shot.

. . . .

[197]

You should have seen me play
last week.

. . . .

[198]
I always choke when money is on the line.

. . . .

[199]
I always aim too far left when
coming out of the bunker.

. . . .

[200]
My arm moved too far to
the left of the vertex.

. . . .

[201]
The rough is way too long.
This is unfair.

. . . .

[202]
I never follow through when trying
to get out of a bunker.

. . . .

[203]

*That golf channel has me
all screwed up.*

55

[204]
I never had a shot-the tree was in the way.

. . . .

[205]
Fore!!!!!!!!

. . . .

[206]
Ever since I made a hole-in-one, I can't concentrate.

. . . .

[207]
My ball was buried in the sand.
Some idiot never raked the trap.

. . . .

[208]
The wind keeps shifting directions. It seems
we are always playing into the wind.

. . . .

[209]
I just can't gauge the chip-shots like I used to.

. . . .

[210]

I can't get my wedge to bite.

. . . .

[211]

I read way too much into the putts.

. . . .

[212]

My back-swing is too flat.

. . . .

[213]

The practice green was much faster.

. . . .

[214]

I need to relax. I'm playing way too fast.

. . . .

[215]

I forgot my umbrella in the car.
Now my glasses are foggy.

. . . .

"Eagle Putt"

[216]

I never saw the break from that angle.

. . . .

[217]

I lifted the tip of the putter too
high off the ground.

. . . .

[218]

I have to go to the bathroom, and I can't
concentrate when I have to go #2.

. . . .

[219]

It's only the eighteenth hole. I'm not
quite warmed up yet.

. . . .

[220]

I never tilted my shoulders.

. . . .

[221]

My angle of impact exceeded the reflection angle, causing me to duff the shot.

[222]

When the hole was moved, the greens-keeper left a gap
in the green. There goes my eagle.

. . . .

[223]

So what if it was a three-footer.
I was only trying to get the ball
close, not make it.

. . . .

[224]

Mulligan!!

. . . .

[225]

There is no port-a-potty, and
I have to go bad.

. . . .

[226]

It's not my swing - it's the clubs!

. . . .

[227]

I just can't generate the power
like when I was young.

. . . .

[228]

Before the sex change, I was allowed to hit from the
red tee. Its just too difficult to score now.

. . . .

[229]

It has been a long week at work and my
boss is a jerk. I can't relax.

. . . .

[230]

All the golf schools I liked
were too expensive - so I self-taught.

. . . .

[231]

My wife is a bitch and she doesn't let me get out, but
she has the money so I put up with her.

. . . .

[232]

I'm getting married in three hours - I can't concentrate.

. . . .

[233]

I usually walk. This "riding in a cart" is not allowing me to get in a groove.

. . . .

[234]

I just want the most strokes for the money - to heck with my score.

. . . .

[235]

My dog chewed a hole in my good golf shoes.

. . . .

[236]

I can't play in 70 degree, sunny weather.
I need snow, wind and rain.

. . . .

[237]

All the weightlifting I am doing has
made me too huge for golf.

. . . .

[238]

My pager vibrated during that putt.

. . . .

[239]

All the photographers' flashbulbs
are throwing off my concentration.
I need to get off the tour.

. . . .

[240]

The slow play throws off my concentration. It
shouldn't take 5 1/2 hours for a round.

. . . .

[241]

I only play well on hilly courses.

. . . .

[242]

I left my new clubs in my other car.

. . . .

[243]

The geese keep following me.
It makes me nervous.

. . . .

[244]

I had to lay up, I was just using
the 3-wood for the heck of it.

. . . .

[245]

My usual golf cart is a Lexus. This one is
uncomfortable-it has no lumbar support.

. . . .

[246]

My usual group is much better than you guys. They
raise my level of play.

. . . .

[247]

I usually use titanium clubs.
These tungsten clubs are too light.

. . . .

[248]

My other driver is a 8.5 degree loft.
I'm losing too much distance out of the box.

. . . .

[249]

In Ireland, they don't count when
I swing and miss.

. . . .

[250]

My ball was resting on a tree stump.

. . . .

[251]

I had a blind shot, but the ball went
where I hit it. I just didn't see the pond.

. . . .

[252]

The lessons I took on the Internet are not working the way they said.

[253]

My ball was wedged in the corner between
the grass and sand. I had no shot.

. . . .

[254]

My country club's fairways are much better.
These conditions are unplayable.

. . . .

[255]

It's too humid. My shirt is sticking to my body.
I need to start wearing deodorant.

. . . .

[256]

My allergies are killing me. I can't
deal with all the pressure.

. . . .

[257]

My regular caddie was arrested. This guy is an idiot-he
doesn't know a 3-wood from a 5-wood.

. . . .

"Sand Play"

[258]
The lie I had wasn't perfectly perfect.

. . . .

[259]
I broke my pitching wedge last time I played. This sand wedge gave me too much loft.

. . . .

[260]
I had the club face opened too much in the bunker.

. . . .

[261]
The greens are too fast. They are like ice.

. . . .

[262]
I can't play with these golf balls. They are all numbered.

. . . .

[263]

I thought if the ball is above
your feet it will slice.

. . . .

[264]

My clubs are too old.
These wooden shafts don't flex.

. . . .

[265]

The chipping area was closed at 3:00 a.m.
(that's when I came to practice).

. . . .

[266]

I just moved to a new house and my back is aching.
I have no follow-through.

. . . .

[267]

I play better with a hard golf ball.
These soft ones are for the pros.

. . . .

[268]

My athlete's foot is causing me to mis-hit.

. . . .

[269]

I keep moving my putter when
I swing my shoulders.

. . . .

[270]

The greens I normally play
on are much slower.

. . . .

[271]

The starter told me to lay up on this hole.
I am a fool for listening.

. . . .

[272]

The ball was wedged up against
the tree. I had no shot.

. . . .

[273]

The grass bunker gave me no shot.
Who the hell designed this course?

. . . .

[274]

My carpet in my living room
doesn't break like this green.

. . . .

[275]

This copper bracelet is too tight on my wrist.
I can't hold on to the club

. . . .

[276]

I keep second-guessing my shots.

. . . .

[277]

Your cigar smoke keeps getting in
my eyes when I putt.

. . . .

[278]

I'm pulling my club back too fast.

. . . .

[279]

There is too much goose crap on the course.

. . . .

[280]

To hell with the tournament. Besides, I don't look
good in green jackets anyway.

. . . .

[281]

I never centered my shaft.

. . . .

[282]

I don't like this gripless club but my broker gave it to me.

. . . .

[283]

The clubs I ordered on the Internet haven't arrived yet.
I'm stuck with these old ones.

. . . .

[284]

The guy on the golf channel hit these
clubs perfect every time. They don't seem
to work for me.

. . . .

[285]

My ball ricocheted off that water pump and went into
the woods. That should be a do-over.

. . . .

[286]

I thought when I turned 40 I could
play from the gold tees.

. . . .

[287]

I can't judge my ball in this cool
December air.

. . . .

[288]

My dog had diarrhea last night.
I didn't get any sleep.

. . . .

[289]

My wife didn't wash my lucky golf shirt.

. . . .

[290]

Titanium balls fly too far for my ability.

. . . .

[291]

From three hundred yards out it looks like the green
sloped away. I should have laid up.

. . . .

[292]

The guys behind us are pushing us.
They are making me nervous.

. . . .

[293]

The snow keeps getting in my eyes.

. . . .

[294]

My pants are too tight - but I think the beer girl likes them.

[295]

There is no way that we are 500 yards out-its only 490.

. . . .

[296]

I had a root canal last year. It still hurts when I golf.

. . . .

[297]

I got whip lash when you started the cart. Now my neck hurts.

. . . .

[298]

I had to take a drop. The speed limit sign was in the way.

. . . .

[299]

I can't golf unless I'm clean-shaven.

. . . .

[300]

I just can't find the sweet spot.

. . . .

[301]

I think my ball is addicted to water.
That's why it keeps landing in the river.

. . . .

[302]

This green isn't fair. It's surrounded
by bunkers.

. . . .

[303]

The Rye grass isn't fair. I can't play
on anything but bluegrass.

. . . .

[304]

The head of my driver fell off
during my swing.

. . . .

[305]

I lost my contact on the last hole.
I'm playing one-eyed.

. . . .

[306]

I have not refilled my medication
this week.

. . . .

[307]

My ball must have hit a sprinkler head. It ended up in
the water. I never go in the water.

. . . .

[308]

I only play well when I bet.

. . . .

[309]

It's too cold to play this morning.
Someone turn up the heat.

. . . .

[310]

*I hate playing on
Sundays. They won't
serve me beer
until 11:00 a.m.*

84

[311]

That putt was short because I'm
using those South American golf balls.
It was one revolution short.

. . . .

[312]

I pulled the putt because an ant
crawled on my shoe.

. . . .

[313]

Hackers tore up the green. I can't play competitively
under these circumstances.

. . . .

[314]

I didn't have a 3 wood so I had
to use my 5 wood.

. . . .

[315]

I thought you said dog-leg left, not right.

. . . .

[316]

I lost the ball in the fog, but it was
headed straight for the green. Someone
must have picked it up.

. . . .

[317]

You were moving when I was
attempting my birdie putt.

. . . .

[318]

When you leaned on your putter, and it left
an indentation on the green.

. . . .

[319]

If the lip on the hole wasn't pushed up it would have fallen.

. . . .

[320]

These are my wife's golf shoes.
Mine are being re-spiked.

. . . .

[321]

My hands are sweaty and the
clubhouse had no soap.

. . . .

[322]

That car door slammed
while I was swinging!

. . . .

[323]

My subscription to that golf
magazine ran out.

. . . .

[324]

I was better before I retired.
I just don't have time to golf anymore.

. . . .

[325]

I drank too much coffee - I have the shakes.

. . . .

[326]

The cable went out at home last night, and
I missed my final lesson on the golf channel.

. . . .

[327]

The ball doesn't fly as far
here in Canada.

. . . .

[328]

My lucky hat is in my wife's car. Otherwise that putt
would have dropped.

. . . .

[329]

I don't like these balls I bought over the
Internet. They fly too far.

. . . .

[330]

The library was out of the golf
teaching magazine.

. . . .

[331]

I have no excuse for that shot. I should have bought
that book by Justin Exner.

. . . .

[332]

My hat is too tight. It's giving me a headache.

. . . .

[333]

My balls need to be cleaned and the
washer is out of water.

. . . .

[334]

The airline ground crew cracked my driver.
I now have to tee off with my 3 wood.

. . . .

[335]

A squirrel picked up my ball and
put it in the bunker.

. . . .

[336]
The GPS on this cart is way off.

. . . .

[337]
That car dealership overcharged me so I
can't afford the good balls.

. . . .

[338]
I can't tee off unless a crowd of
people is watching.

. . . .

[339]
The alarm on my watch went off
during my back-swing.

. . . .

[340]
I only par holes with white flags.

. . . .

[341]

*The dew on the green
slowed up my putt.*

[342]

I forgot to take my vitamins this morning.
Now I'm out of energy.

. . . .

[343]

Your cell phone should have been turned off.
I want a do-over.

. . . .

[344]

I need yellow lenses for my sunglasses. I'm getting too
many ultraviolet rays.

. . . .

[345]

I thought this little shark on my shirt
made me play better.

. . . .

[346]

I'm exhausted - the batteries in my TV
remote died yesterday.

. . . .

[347]

My thumb wasn't aligned
with the club's axis.

. . . .

[348]

I never looked at the whole green.
It slopes left.

. . . .

[349]

The shade of that tree got in my eyes.

. . . .

[350]

I never aligned the club face
on my set-up.

. . . .

[351]

I can't play unless I have sex
prior to playing.

. . . .

[352]

I have sarcoidosis, I haven't
been able to play.

. . . .

[353]

One of my shoelaces broke on the back-swing.

. . . .

[354]

I haven't been able to play since the auto
accident. I can't sue for strokes.

. . . .

[355]

I can't focus on golf when my
football team is playing.

. . . .

[356]

I spread my legs too far and I couldn't see my balls-I
mean ball.

. . . .

[357]

I just can't envision the shot - and that's
the key to the whole game.

. . . .

[358]

Your golf shirt is too bright.
Who the hell dresses you?

. . . .

[359]

I never flared my left foot.

. . . .

[360]

The club only had small buckets
available at the range. I needed a large.

. . . .

[361]

I teed the ball too low.

. . . .

[362]

Since breaking up with her, my house is
dirty, so are my clothes, and so are my balls-
I can't concentrate with dirty balls.

. . . .

[363]

I can't concentrate since I got fired
from the orange juice factory.

. . . .

[364]

Its much windier on the west coast. I need at least 30
knots to play properly.

. . . .

[365]

The sun dried out the green.
The balls are rolling too fast.

. . . .

[366]

Polo is my strong game.

. . . .

[367]

I can only make the 10-footers; the
3-footers throw me off.

. . . .

[368]

I should have focused on the spot
behind the ball.

. . . .

[369]

I was in Seattle the last three weeks and all it did was
rain. I couldn't practice.

. . . .

[370]

Since filing for bankruptcy, I can only
golf twice a week.

. . . .

[371]

I thought blue markers meant 100 yards.

. . . .

[372]

This Alzheimer's makes me forget
where my ball landed.

. . . .

[373]

I only started playing last month.

. . . .

[374]

I can't golf regularly for religious reasons.

. . . .

[375]

I thought the right hand was
supposed to be on top when I putt.

. . . .

[376]

I thought the white stake on the side is
what I was aiming for. I didn't realize it
was out of bounds.

. . . .

"Foot Wedge"

[377]

*My body is swaying
too much
from the alcohol.*

[378]
I swung down on the ball.

. . . .

[379]
My feet must not have been
parallel to the target.

. . . .

[380]
I moved my right knee on the back-swing, creating an
illusion of power
which was improperly assessed.

. . . .

103

[381]
Since shooting 68, I haven't been able to break 100.

. . . .

[382]
I can't afford golf lessons.

. . . .

[383]

My body tipped forward on the back-swing which
opened the face of the 3-wood,
creating a slice.

. . . .

[384]

I was bent too far forward over the
ball to get spin on it.

. . . .

[385]

These new balls suck.
I only like playing with range balls.

. . . .

[386]

My tee had a crack in it. I usually only buy
stuff made in the USA.

. . . .

[387]

My ball landed in a fairway divot because some lazy-
butt didn't replace his divot.

. . . .

[388]

The greens-keeper aerated the fairways
too early in the season. I can't get
any roll on the ball.

. . . .

[389]

I had a clump of mud on my ball,
causing it to spin to the left.

. . . .

[390]

The video golf instruction tape I purchased didn't
teach me how to putt.

. . . .

[391]

The driving range wouldn't let me use
any of my woods, only irons.

. . . .

[392]

I'm out of tees, but I have a bunch at home.

. . . .

"Are We Playing Winter Rules?"

[393]

The only tree on the entire hole and
I have hit it twice.

. . . .

[394]

The water in the creek wasn't this high last week. That
would have been a great shot.

. . . .

[395]

I had my knees bent too far and I got
way under the ball.

. . . .

[396]

I'm getting old. I used to beat you all
the time when you were kids.

. . . .

[397]

My putter shaft is bent.

. . . .

[398]

My ball has a scuff on it from hitting the pin on the last par-3. Now it spins too much around its axis.

[399]

I haven't had time to practice my putting.

. . . .

[400]

I never noticed this trap before.
I usually hit the green from 275 out.

. . . .

[401]

I bent my 9-iron while killing a pig
for the roast for my 22nd birthday party
so I had to use my wedge.

. . . .

[402]

This putter stinks. It has no lines
on it to set up the putt.

. . . .

[403]

I need a beer and the beer cart lady
hasn't been around.

. . . .

[404]

My short game is my strong suit, not driving.

. . . .

[405]

On impact my hips went through
too early and it opened up my swing,
causing the ball to angle improperly.

. . . .

[406]

I put way too much spin on the ball and
it rolled off the green, over the hill, bounced
off that rake and fell into the trap.

. . . .

[407]

I usually play with the club pro, but he
isn't here to give me tips.

. . . .

[408]

The wind blew my skirt up into my face.

. . . .

[409]

I took too much of a divot. It caused the ball
to fall short of the 125 yards required.

. . . .

[410]

I pulled my club too far back on the back-swing,
creating insufficient torque on the
forward transition.

. . . .

[411]

The beer cart girl went home. I can't relax.

. . . .

[412]

I opened the face of the club.
It must be the cast.

. . . .

[413]

Those damn people won't shut up.

. . . .

[414]

I only read three angles to the putt. I should have
taken all four. I'm too lazy.

. . . .

[415]

I just choked. Again..

. . . .

[416]

The ball just broke too much to the left.

. . . .

[417]

That leaf blew in front of my putt!

. . . .

[418]

I rotated my hands too far to the left,
which made the club face open at an
improper point of the swing.

. . . .

"My Hero"

[419]
My cat tinkled on my golf glove,
so I can't use it.

. . . .

[420]
I aimed my shoulder too far left of the target.

. . . .

[421]
I was standing too close to the ball.

. . . .

[422]
I didn't flex my wrists on the back-swing.

. . . .

[423]
I just don't know what the hell I'm doing wrong.

. . . .

[424]
I must need new glasses.

. . . .

[425]

I have really bad jock itch so my
stance is all screwed up.

. . . .

[426]

My hair gel evaporated and now my
hair keeps getting in my eyes.

. . . .

[427]

I was kicked off of my high school golf team because I
kept fondling the balls. I haven't played since. It's too
emotionally painful.

. . . .

[428]

It hurts too much to practice,
with the war injury and all.

. . . .

[429]

The golf seminar I wanted to go to was sold out.

. . . .

[430]

I can't get my mental checklist
in its proper order.

. . . .

[441]

My dog ran away this morning
so I didn't have time to warm up.

. . . .

[432]

It's so humid, I came out of the trap on the last
hole and the wind blew the sand in my face
and now it's stuck and I can't see.

. . . .

[433]

I play for the exercise, not the score.

. . . .

[434]

I can only get enthusiastic about sex.
Golf just doesn't do it so I don't try.

. . . .

[435]

After that last shot, I'm just too embarrassed
to try and hit the ball.

. . . .

[436]

I get so excited when I play, I can't relax.
I love this game!

. . . .

[437]

My underwear is soiled from when that guy's ball
almost hit me. It's very distracting.

. . . .

[438]

The leaky faucet at my mistress's
home kept me up all night.

. . . .

[439]

I just can't get that triple bogey out of my head.

. . . .

"What Rain?"

[440]
My brother took my good golf glove.

. . . .

[441]
Just to beat my score, my father
gave me hollow golf balls.

. . . .

[442]
My calculator must have run out of
batteries. Put me down for a three.

. . . .

[443]
I am constantly over-judging my shots.

. . . .

[444]
I am committed to my wife.
Golf has always come second.

. . . .

[445]

I only care if I look good, not how I golf.

. . . .

[446]

I only took the game up to get away from the wife. I
don't really care if I'm good.

. . . .

[447]

I only play for the camaraderie.

. . . .

[448]

Since I got the implants, my swing
just isn't the same.

. . . .

[449]

My lucky argyles are in my other golf bag.
I can't putt without them.

. . . .

[450]

I just don't play well in the sun, rain, clouds, snow or
sleet-I lose my focus.

. . . .

[451]

I can never get my last shot off my mind.

. . . .

[452]

My ex-girlfriend's brother-in-law is an
old golf pro. He use to give me free golf lessons. If we
would have stayed together,
I could have made that putt.

. . . .

[453]

I only play for personal, non-substantive goals.

. . . .

[454]

Golf isn't fun if it's competitive,
so I don't try hard.

. . . .

[455]

The warden wouldn't let me practice
all those years in prison.

. . . .

[456]

I usually just play the slice. Now I'm hitting
it straight. I just don't understand this game.

. . . .

[457]

I never even saw that tree next to
the pond next to the forest.

. . . .

[458]

I thought the red stakes were a
target towards the green.

. . . .

[459]

My cat chewed up my Thursday golf
underwear. Now I have to wear Sunday's.

. . . .

[460]

I didn't put on my deodorant this morning and the smell is making my eyes water.

[461]

Some idiot ahead of us keeps leaving
sunflower seeds on the green.

. . . .

[462]

I thought this was a par six.
I was just laying up.

. . . .

[463]

I'm not wearing my lucky golf strap.

. . . .

[464]

There are no ball washers on this whole course. I can't
play with dirty balls.

. . . .

[465]

My ex-girlfriend used to iron all my socks. I just can't
do it the way she did them, damnit.

. . . .

[466]

I don't care how I score when I'm young.
My only goal is to live long enough
to shoot lower than my age.

. . . .

[467]

I haven't had sex all month. I just can't putt.
I have no control of my stick.

. . . .

[468]

I was surrounded by trees.

. . . .

[469]

I need one of those shark grips on my putter.
It seems to work for all the guys on the tour.

. . . .

[470]

The ball broke uphill. There must
be a lake beyond that river.

. . . .

[471]

I thought you aim halfway when
chipping with a 7 iron.

. . . .

[472]

I dropped my left shoulder and hooked the ball.

. . . .

[473]

Bermuda grass sucks.
My club keeps getting stuck.

. . . .

[474]

I can only chip with an 8 iron. I must have
left it on the last hole, or maybe you are
trying to sabotage my round.

. . . .

[475]

My calves hurt from running.

. . . .

[476]

I shot a 71 on this course last time. Then again, it was on my computer.

[477]

I played too much softball last week,
I'm hitting the ball too flat.

. . . .

[478]

I picked up my foot on my backswing.

. . . .

[479]

My tempo is off since the incident
with the ball washer.

. . . .

[480]

I usually hit the driver off the fairway fine.
The greens-keeper must be doing a poor job.

. . . .

[481]

I can only get motivated to play golf
after watching "Caddyshack."

. . . .

[482]

I should have put more iron on the ball.

. . . .

[483]

I need to change my putting technique.

. . . .

[484]

It was easier to putt when I wasn't good.
Now it's just too much pressure.

. . . .

[485]

Golf is about etiquette,
not playing well.

. . . .

[486]

These sneakers just don't get me the proper support
required for my ankles.

. . . .

[487]

I'm used to playing courses with pine trees.
The oaks are distracting.

. . . .

[488]

I putted really well on the miniature
golf course last night.

. . . .

[489]

I'm gripping the club way too hard.

. . . .

[490]

I should have used the putter
to get out of the bunker.

. . . .

[491]

That duct tape just doesn't work
as well as real grips.

. . . .

[492]

My golf bag is too small.
I usually have a larger selection of clubs.

. . . .

[493]

The tee box has no grass in it. I only play
well at well-manicured courses.

. . . .

[494]

I'm only playing for the charity.

. . . .

[495]

What do you mean, winter rules
aren't allowed in the summer?

. . . .

[496]

I didn't come to play golf. I wanted to
see the Cub's spring training.

. . . .

[497]

The airline lost my bags.
Again.

[498]

These clubs are instruments
of torture - I hate this game.

. . . .

[499]

I'm used to playing in Alaska.
When I hit the pond, it's usually frozen.
This isn't fair.

. . . .

[500]

I'm dehydrated from the heat.

. . . .

[501]

I'm used to playing night golf.
This daytime stuff confuses me.

. . . .

Do you have any excuses of your own?

You can send your best excuses to us via our website at www.501excuses.com

If you provide us with an original excuse that we use in our next book, we'll send you a free copy of it!

Look for Justin's next book

501 Excuses to go Golfing

*Arriving soon at your
favorite bookstore*

Order additional copies of this book for your family and friends!

Call toll-free (800) 932-5420

or

Send us your name, address and phone number, with a check for $10 per book payable to 501Excuses to:

Golf Excuses Book
P.O. Box 811252
Cleveland, OH 44181-1252

or order at
www.501excuses.com

For information on freelance artistry by Dawn M. Emerson or for help publishing your book, please call Greenleaf Enterprises, Inc. at (800) 932-5420.

139